UNPUNCTUATED AWE

# UNPUNCTUATED AWE

## POEMS OF SANTA FE

*Joan Logghe*

Sylvia ~
This is the birthday
of the world.
♡
Joan
Logghe

TRES CHICAS BOOKS

THESE POEMS PREVIOUSLY APPEARED IN PRINT OR ON-LINE
WITH THANKS TO THE FOLLOWING:

"April in Santa," letterpress chapbook by Tom Leech and the Press at the Palace
of the Governors. "Arrivistes" and "Arranged Marriage," Chokecherries:
SOMOS Anthology 2012. "Still, Life With Datura" and "Jack Gilbert Comes
to the Lensic," Chokecherries 20 Years Anniversary Edition, 2013. "Pioneer,"
Adobe Wall #1. "The Deep End," Malpais Review #3. "Mattachine in
El Rancho," 200 New Mexico Poems on-line publication for the Centennial and
forthcoming UNM Press. "Music on the Plaza," Santa Fe 400, Questions and
Answers, Sunstone Press, Edited by Elizabeth West. "Rain Business,"
Sin Fronteras. Poetry Posts, Project by Miriam Sagan at Santa Fe Community
College. "Kitchen Sink" and "President's Day" in Centennial Issue of
Malpais Review. "Sitting Still for Beauty," El Palacio Magazine: Art, History,
and Culture of the Southwest. "Drought" and "At Gathering for Mother Earth,"
New Mexico Mercury on-line. "Unpunctuated Awe," in Odes & Offerings,
Sunstone Press and Sage Green Journal on-line.

COVER PHOTOGRAPH: Dianne Schwartz

BRUSH PAINTINGS: Joan Logghe

BOOK DESIGN: JB Bryan / La Alameda Press

Set in Poliphilus with Blado italic

Tres Chicas Books
P.O. Box 417
El Rito, New Mexico 87530

"When it's over
I'm going to be like nobody
all over the place."

OCTOBER 2011


"I was so quotable
I had to write myself down."

FEBRUARY 2012
@ Tune Up Café

# CONTENTS

# Where, When, and Why I Took Note

In June 2012, after two years serving as the city's poet, I handed out letterpress copies of my poem, "April in Santa" to the city council. I had written it the previous year for the council. Tom Leech and James Bourland made it a beautiful hand sewn chapbook. The Mayor proclaimed it JOAN LOGGHE DAY and read the proclamation. I answered by reading a poem, one I had written for the Nava Elementary School's 6th grade "Continuation Ceremony."

I walked out of the city hall, spilled onto Marcy Street and felt oddly out of body. I had to sit on a bench and regain myself. Had to go eat spicy yellowtail sushi. Somebody should have told me this was my "Continuation." I felt rode hard and put away wet as my rodeo cowboy neighbor once said about a horse we had. I was entering Post-Poet Laureateville, a tricky terrain.

A few months later my friend Carolyn came up to me on Grant Avenue and said, "Hi. Didn't you used to be somebody?" Then she regretted saying that, but in truth she was giving voice to how I secretly felt. I was again a pilgrim and a stranger in this place, after feeling that I had a key to the city, or at very least had treated myself to a key to its parking meters so I would not scramble for quarters during my tenure as city poet.

During the two years serving the city I had written one hundred poems, some of which make this book. Poems were written for the famed Pancake Breakfast on the Fourth of July, for Labor Day, for political action on the Santa Fe River, for mayor David Coss' State of the City address, for Santa Fe High graduation keynote, and for two Valentine's Day visits to local nursing homes.

I wrote on site at the Community Gallery, at Indian Market on the Plaza, and at S.O.F.A., a very hip Sculptural Objects Functional

Art. I wrote in schools and on the RailRunner train heading south. The city was rife with poetry — if only I had my notebook I could write it down. I stood in the New Mexico Museum of Art in awe of Gustave Baumann on Free Fridays. I wrote in restaurants and when I should have been listening at the Lensic. I wrote with students at Capshaw Middle School, New Mexico School for the Arts, and the Santa Fe Girls' School where I have been a poet-in-residence for 14 years. I never have had such a totally fun and productive time. I was doing what I was supposed to do for my creative imperative. In terms of poetry, it was as inspirational as heartbreak and a lot more fun.

What ensued were a series of occasional poems, a genre usually reserved for a wedding, a birthday, or a funeral. I wrote for a city. So, here I invite you to celebrate Santa Fe with me. I am smitten. I own this town. I defend it when anyone maligns. However, I hasten to say I have never lived in town. We settled on the northern edge of Santa Fe County, good enough for poet laureate requirements. I also worked in town, over 30 years visiting its many schools, running an open mic at Center for Contemporary Arts, teaching a bit at the Community College, and giving hundreds of readings over the years. So, do I rest on my so-called laurels and settle in, or keep on trucking? I used to be somebody. Now that I rejoin Emily Dickinson as Nobody, I can get on with my work, family, and life.

# A GESTURE OF SKY

*"Accept that Santa Fe isn't just tacos and turquoise anymore, and you'll find yourself loving the New Mexican capital not for what it was, but what it is."*
*Fred Bernstein, New York Times, May 23, 2010*

The gesture of the daylily is to go orange
then to dry, a muted version of itself.
A gesture of clouds, imagine every white thing
you've ever seen in your life and layer them
above Santa Fe. That is just today, now
multiply by all the days in a year, then a decade,
then 400 years of clouds with no conquerors.
This is the gesture of sky. Rain here
can be masculine or feminine.
I prefer the gentle.

## Music on the Plaza

*dedicated to David Lescht*

Then there was that evening on Plaza Fatima,
little circle tucked between Acequia  Madre
and Canyon Road.  Behind the ravens settling down
for night, beneath the scent of basil and roses
we could hear the music from the Plaza, free

music filling in the distance, traveling up
Paseo de Peralta and turning left and music
turning right at Delgado and right again, and we heard
as if from long times ago, a tune. We stopped,
put down our pens, our water glasses filled

with juice of watermelon, and we either wept
or smiled, depending on how our families
found themselves that season.  Myself, I strained
to hear and then leaned back, received.
This city has been my Santa Fe for years, holy

as we ourselves are music. I've driven streets and faith,
walked more than a few miles. Music for the meals
I've eaten, grace notes for the friends I've made.
I ate my first enchilada at The Shed. Red.
I met men with languages I speak and those
whose language I can't.  Men with state jobs and

at my bank, my money floating in and out
of hands, tellers, Josephine, now gone, she was

rooting for me.　My shopping life, the goods
and　jewelry, my taxes going for the public good.
That music.　Every time I buy a stamp downtown,
this music　from the Plaza, this town grown city
right before my years.　That music from the bandstand
that summer night. That night, the voice of city.

# The Passing of the Pencil Ceremony

"I am so proud of you.  Don't lose a bit of it."
*Kaylee Logghe, age 4*


Last night on the Plaza I danced .
The Plaza was painted by Breughel.
The man who bought my mother's car was there.

There was flirting as befits a summer night.
The drinks were stronger than they had any right.
My grandkids were lively as salt on the rim.

Last night on the plaza they sang.
I wanted a blue guitar like anything.
The mayor was there and the St. Bernard

Of my childhood friend.  She rescued
The dog, night rescued the music from the air.
I wanted a dancer's body and more time.

Sangria is the name of a body of blood.
Last night on the plaza I made a mistake.
This is weeks before Fiesta and already

The mariachis are coming down Palace Ave.
We have to move aside in wonder.
Is it possible to be too alive?

# On Site at S.O.F.A.

"You still have that new Poet Laureate smell."
*Kenneth Johnson SWIA jeweler*

The thing about growing old in Santa Fe
is you can walk downtown with your heart dry.
Your arroyo heart ready and waiting for flood.
You are washed away by the love of art.

And you're old, so your open fourth chakra
fills with art, things you can't afford but maybe
you spring anyhow, because your art filled heart
is always spring and you don't want to run off anymore

with the artist, just happy to be moved to random acts
of writing on the bench in the midst of sculpture.
In full tilt love, even now, and that way the hinges
never rust, that newly minted smell of a woman fallen

always, as you rise to every occasion of art⁄heart,
a Santa Fe disease, and with your hair grown O'Keeffe white,
walk this city land⁄filled with art, which isn't so far from holy faith.
If you stop and look at it, so close to silver July skies.

## Twenty Miles Home

In the O'Keeffe Café I say, "I'm a local"
And the waitress says, "Welcome to Santa Fe."

This city shines me like jewelry
On my right arm, a gift from a writer.
This silver cuff cut out into the pattern
Of rams' horns and always complimented.

I say, this was a gift from a friend
Who lives in Raton and even though
I rarely see her,
Even though I get irritable with myself

Even then on my right arm letting
The words move under it shiny and even
When swimming laps or braiding my hair
Whiter by the day, this city shines at night.

Home, I can carry my turquoise library card
With the words in white. I can call it home
I've never lived in, this silver city, this lilac
In spring, this Russian sage in summer,

Bandstand free each evening. A place
I never abandon, when the tourists come
They are as lonely as I was in Venice,
When arroyos flood I have to drive them.

This city with its stores of jewelry and clay,
Any day at all you can find me with the bracelet
From Taxco given by a friend, that even the drugstore
Girl, from Mexico herself, admires.

I take it off
So she can hold it, put her young energy
Into it, like an old city with a new neighborhood,
Like telling someone you can see their best faults.

# Spanish Market

Made new friend from Lubbock, under the clouds
thick as Apocalypse. Ate cake at the Zia, might
as well at the end of time. Sunnier now.

My well fed blood, thunder under life,
chocolate and mariachi, all manner
of glorious — Santa Fe day at Market.

Making the rounds of old friends,
Rose of Chimayo and Beatrice Maestas Sandoval
of *colcha*. Taught me old embroidery tradition.

We are this fabric of loose threads, *sabanía*, fine
and hand spun. I sit behind the table with Camilla,
out of the rain, dear friend of mica and clay.

I'll write a poem behind micaceous pots, earth,
sky, money, music, chocolate cake at Zia.
No mas and everything. Mañanitas

from the bandstand sung by a child.
Always one more major beauty
in this plaza of rain and hanging flowers.

I kiss Roger Montoya, visit René Zamora.
Señor Ancheta not rained out.
Names are dropping, beautiful names full of water.

I buy, finally, a flaming heart
of recycled computer circuitry from a friend
of decades, Marion Martinez, blessing me.

Just when I think one more great thing
couldn't happen I hear, then see,
belly dancers at the corner of Water and Galisteo.

Young woman I taught at the Girls' School.
Tribal dance of a serious depth and holy hips. Tattoo
on her shoulder, "Peace of mind. It's a piece of cake."

## The Deep End

The aspens' white bark
Their leaves small for desert.
I conserve water. I conserve nothing.
I shop as if it could kill me.

Something will kill me.  Last week
at the funeral it was so private.
Finally a thing I won't talk about.
How did I get here from aspens

on Read Street to aspens on Camino
Santander?  The woman was a swimming
pool friend.  She and an older man
vied for the deep corner at exercise class.

They both died last week, Rose Marie and Herman.
I even woke dreaming of her in her wheelchair.
I read he was a member of Sierra Club.
Death itself seems fragile, though final.

Last week the dogs barked and it was hot.
Tonight, so still and blissfully cool. I forgot
to sing.  All week I forgot how it was to be
so alive it comes out your throat.

The cell phone sounds like rain.
It doesn't bother me, nor did the barking dogs
last week. We can write in two directions, life
and death, past and future, aspens and aspens.

## Labor Day Poem

The best job I ever had was driving a school bus
right out of college and I thought it a job suitable
for a poet, cruising the upscale Pittsburgh suburb
in a Blue Bird bus.

The best job I ever had was Chicago, teaching kindergarten,
the kids in the morning and the kids in the afternoon.
I taught them the hora and the Mexican Hat Dance
and Woody Guthrie. Even now, all in their 40's
they wonder where they got these tunes.

The best job I ever had was San Francisco, working
in a firehouse with the lost children. Every staff meeting
we'd disagree about how to hold the children when they
couldn't hold themselves. That was a job I walked to
past a corner bakery on 9th and Judah that sold pirogues.

The best job was Wisconsin, your family's dairy farm
of fifty cows and your childhood.
I was the new wife, scraped calf pens,
we got paid in house and milks and eggs.

The best job I ever had was White Rock, selling
geraniums and snap dragons, my first truck
with bedding plants. 1973, I watered nursery trees,
carried bags of steer manure to cars. I learned
to say maybe you watered it too much, or maybe too little.

The best job was not substitute teaching.
I got the spitballs and the thumbtacks on my chair.

The best job was waiting tables at El Paragua in Española
My old boss still knows me, says, "Oh Joanie, I remember
when you dropped the steak and lobster." And I recall
the sopapilla basket I set on fire, too close to the candle.
But even then I felt the joy of work and customers
treated us as humans not as servants, but still I tip well
in homage to those days.

In Santa Fe, on Canyon Road, I swept the patio
in my apron as the tourist bus passed by the Haven.
I tried to look like local color. Then I was a chiropractor's
right hand until my third child came onto the scene, I mean,
I was a mother almost all along and that was a hidden
love and job of work.

And all along I gave my life to poetry, which begs
the question, am I management or labor? Thirty years
and here I stand. I always thought if I aimed low,
kept my feet on solid earth, I'd be myself for the long haul.
My self. Best job I ever had.

# ARRANGED MARRIAGE

In the late afternoon the music comes down from the balcony. A boy
dressed as a banana rides his skateboard. A juggler balances
on a pink ball. I get that feeling again, this is my city.

Today Alex called from the mountains. His cell phone
took me to the aspens and he said he could see
the alluvial plains. He could see the Sandias, the Ortiz.

How much he loves, he was rhapsodic, we both
praised our luck. He said, *I want to get down on my knees.*
*Give thanks.* We both ended up

here and made a go. I walked across the Plaza
with my inhalations of music and the sun about ready to give
its famous glow before nodding off.

I walked across the plaza and hugged Tim.
His braid down his back, his heart full of children and poetry.
I heard the music coming from the balcony as if I were in Seville

as if I would next be hugging Lorca, because anything
can happen in this place. I knew the woman I met last week
was under the portal with her family from Santo Domingo.

I knew that my blood was rinsed here by wind,
by the mountains breathing, by walking across
the plaza, with the music coming down from the balcony.

It could have been any century if I forgot the pavement
and forgave, if we all let go of victims and conquerors.
If music were religion, if you saw the daytime moon.

I didn't leave until late.  By then it was dark and the music
was still falling, there was clapping and the man still balancing
on the pink ball, tossing bowling pins into the air.

## At the O'Keeffe

I am standing by the chalk
crumbled and soft colors
of sandstone.

The yellow especially,
chalk dust after a day
of hiking, showing off
the lay of the land.

I am standing by papers
carefully labeled
by paint brushes bundled and held by a rubber band

and paint brushes fanned out flat
pointing at me, saying
in sixteen voices,
do your work.

I am standing  by paint inside the
leather case, opened
cadmium red, deep
finest paint Grubacher

cobalt blue, deep,
I am standing 18 inches
from linseed oil.
Hooker's green next to vermillion,

cadmium green
standing by flake white
the largest tube.  It takes
plenty of white to catch these skies.

Light is dimmed in a museum
for conservation. "Canyon
with Crows." "Blue Flower."
"Red Mesa." Out of these tubes.

"Holding Bones in 1937,"
ten years before I was standing.
The chalk dust finds a way
into my chest,

The rocks in the basket,
the rocks in the bowl
the rocks on a plate. "Red Hills"
and "White Flower," hers, part mine.

Blue sky with flaming gold cottonwood.
Blue morning was
mine. White morning of dreams.

Horse skull, bone
"Horse Skull with Roses," oil.
"White Place,"
"Black Place," home, stone.

In her Model A, Ghost Ranch
through a car window.
Ten years before I stood here
she held brushes.

We crossed paths finally
in 1978, I sat one row behind her
famous head in Chimayo, Holy Cross, at a wedding.

Then my twenty-five years at the Ranch
I painted her alive. She rung
the bells of color
flawless, and flowers.

"Took a lot of guts
to see things this way and let
other people know
you were seeing it."

Faithful to her paint
and her canvas, she fled
and led me here to stand by her chalk
cliffs. Especially the yellows.
Chunks of thick broken, color.

## At Northern

Northern New Mexico College, Eng 112.C
Carrie Vogel's composition class


What I know about Espanola is that I'll never be a local
not even when I die here, not even if I have three
local kids and three local grandkids. I'll always
have Pittsburgh in me, streetcars and sooty skies.

Even wearing turquoise there will be smoke
around me. My husband is more local than I am.
He is a local through pure loco.
He was a fireman retired from the fire.
He is a farmer with no cows. He is a guy
with a pickup truck and a yellow plate.
He chose yellow because he is a real New Mexican
who gave his life here. Hey, I did too. I drove the highway;
I paid land tax and taxes on my clothing.
I cried enough tears to grow a tamale,
an enchilada, a cholla and a bandana.

I laughed enough laughs here to adopt a section of road.
say between La Puebla and Chimayo
on the curve into tomorrow. I am transplanted cilantro,
ready to flavor the salsa. And ready to bolt. No,
I am a tomato that just got the freeze.

# SCIENCE CLASS

I.

Clouds covered the camera lens and I was obscured.
Clouds sit on the mountain saturated.
Clouds mending the fences between day and night.
Clouds turn my head and I apply for a scholarship
to heaven. Clouds on the Sangrés, clouds on
the Jemez. Today is solid clouds and I am
a cloudy woman. Clouds inside a science class.
Clouds wearing lipstick and blush, clouds trotting
around the sky saying "Cumulus."
Raunchy clouds, cowboy clouds,
clouds riding bareback on white or gray horses.
Stacatto clouds dappling the sky, fish scale
clouds refusing to take the hook. Did I mention
clouds? Out loud and proud. Cirrus and thunderheads,
rain looms called by their other name, virga.
Clouds which sound loud
but are usually silent.

2.

I halted, all the energy of preparation shone
onto students' hands rising and ideas
flowing over their heads,
moving from them towards me.

They were studying speed. I was accelerated.
I spoke with velocity. There was no friction as often
occurs in classrooms of this size.

Kinetic as playground antics the thoughts
flew to and from, you to me to you and a solid
happiness fell towards me, heavy as a ball
called by gravity.

A water balloon
about to burst. But first, let me tell you
who you are, and then you tell me
who I am and in instantaneous free-fall

we are all poetic scientists and scientific
poets and genius comes with a Eureka,
an Aha! Temperature dropping
and so we pass in the halls, another fall day

3.

Babies born in the night have brown eyes,
daytime babies have blue.

Watermelon is 90% water. Gravity kept the water
in the sea, but it keeps trying to escape.
Instead of sleep, she lived on soup.

The proof of the pudding is in the evening
not the eating.  I was told that a stitch in time
saves nine but what happens to ten?

This side of the night is brighter than that side.
A horse running after a train is always a math word problem.

Inhaling, the flowers breathed out while she breathed in.
Until you left home, I didn't know quiet.

The birds have an alibi for why they were late to school.
Gravity is second cousin to the grizzly bear.

Speeding up time is possible if you're a magician,
but not if you're a mother.

being a mother is scientific.  Being a student is holy work
like being a nun or a monk. Science is made of light bulbs.

4.

Are thin rivers happier than fat ones?
Can the river here live again in winter?
Is several less than a couple and is a dozen enough?
How come it isn't time to dance when I have so much music in me?
Are you sure the schools are filled with students and not with silver?
Isn't it amazing how caterpillars wear outfits
of black and yellow, but grubs only wear gray.?
Are we about to wake up and find butterflies in this poem?
Is a poem a lapsed song?
Which came first, white or night?
How come the silence of writing is hushed as a prayer?
Will they kick me out of class if I say the word holy?

## SELF PORTRAIT AT GIRLS' SCHOOL

In the self portrait of the woman
who isn't me, it's possible I could relax,
step out of this body, drift
the brain away, look into blue
eyes, shell the peas of thought, string
the beans of direction, put the clock
in one pocket and the compass
in the other.  Chalk the air,
pool cue, sidewalk, blackboard.

I'm a day away from her. We cleared the land
behind our house. She would walk there without
being out of breath. Is my heart breathing
her in, those turquoise eyes, that round
face with a wimple? She says,
"Yes, and don't cave in and articulate
your destinations, set fantastic goals,
live a fanciful life." Sigh, for she
gives me the place underneath a yawn.

All done, gone, gone, and gone.
She says, "head and heart." She says "Encircle
my face with paint. Deliver colors to me
an inevitable painted dawn."

# SNOW DAY

Prince of Peace delayed two hours,
Crownpoint and Gallup Public, Hobbs Municipal
all delayed. Pecos Valley closed. Battaan, Mountain
Academy, Bernalillo, Bosque, all delayed.

School of Dreams Academy, I did not make this up,
Sierra Blanca, Hope Christian, Horizon West.
Silver Consolidated School, Immanuel, Jemez Valley,
two hours. Sky City Community School, South Valley.

Academy de Esperanza, Laguna all delayed two hours.
Saint Bonaventure, Thoreau, buses delayed, Lovington,
Saint Michaels, Saint Pius, Saint Thomas Aquinas.
Sunset Mesa, Taos Day, the schools scrolled across

the bottom of the screen. Tatum Municipal
staff must report. The Tutorial, Mora and Moriarity,
imagine the students dreaming late, Tierra Encantado,
All staff report. Tohatchi, Village Academy.

West Las Vegas closed. Wagon Mound no evening
activity. Santa Fe delay. Institute of American Indian Arts
delayed. Luna Community College, Albuquerque
Academy, Albuquerque Public and Sandia Prep.

But nothing about my neighborhood, sweet Pojoaque,
Española, places north. So I sweep the snow and go.

# THE BLANK PAGE IS THE SNOW

*For teachers Deborah Hawthorne and Eric Druva*


The twelve children
still in school on a day of raging snow
know the words simile, alliteration, onomatopoeia.
Accumulates is my favorite verb. Their teacher
wears suspenders and a tie. His hair slick
as black ice. It's Black and White Day at school.
Meanwhile incessant, flashing veils of snow,

out the window.  Each child knows something
they didn't know they knew. The silence
of writing is like snow. Both are rare in school.
The art teacher falls in love with the moment.
The morning is long as empty playground hours.
The boy says his grandmother is a clock.  The snow
is old, it is Navajo snow, Sangre de Cristos are gone

in snow.  The loud speaker breaks in.  Early dismissal.
No basketball, no cheerleaders, no this, no that.
Pretty soon everyone is speaking in poetry. They draw
in black on white, like a magpie on chain link. The art
teacher finds a magpie on-line, dressed formally.
I pilfer language, gather bits and specks, as it accumulates
from our brilliant snow-blown minds.

## WRITING UNDER THE INFLUENCE

It doesn't get much better than this,
two snow days, but the natural gas ran out.

Protest in the streets of Egypt
but maybe freedom around the bloody corner.

Snow again right now. I've forgotten to taste
the snowflakes. This one minty with newness,

this one radioactive, this one genetically modified.
Julia from Russia plays piano as the girls ballroom dance.

Things people are not talking about: greed, empire,
oligarchy, a conspiracy of weather.

A veil of snow between here and those mountains.
It doesn't get much better than this.

You meeting me for lunch of enchiladas
at the Sopapilla Factory. Forty years we've driven

to meet up, driving each other crazy and sane,
this polishing act we married into.

Seriously, my grandson says, Actually. It is as good
as anybody on Planet Earth, Turtle Island, Gaia, ever will get.

# INTERSECTION

*For Santa Fe High Graduation Keynote*


Here I stand at the intersection of Yucca and Siringo,
between Zia and tomorrow,
with my too many words and my disguise as a gray haired poet.

Here you sit in your cap and gowns,
at the intersection of heart and mind,
at the corner of past and future, right now.

And here we are with the mystery of how things turn out,
with the mornings all groggy with too late and too early,
with the getting to high school anyway, with your homework

done or the pages still printing, with the many lessons learned
and the already forgotten stored inside you. With your success
and the blessing of Santa Fe all around us, its sky

which has been smiling for centuries, watching you,
its paved promises and is been-there-done-that. With its dreams,
graffiti tagged illegally onto your souls.

With its history as complicated as any place.
Just yesterday I was driving south on Saint Francis at Cordova
and I heard drumming. Through my closed car window, drumming,

with its base note of Pueblo people, deep drumming
through the open window of a car shining silver,
feathers hung from its rear view mirror.

And the language spoken was English with a back story
of Tewa and a Spanish flamenco, just yesterday with its Conquistadors
and the conquered and nobody giving up.

That's what I love, a city where nobody gives up.
I am dreaming of red shoes, red with sunset, with blood, with a taste of
drama and never stop the dancing.

With your future all shiny like WET PAINT DON'T TOUCH,
with your unknown and your planned.  With just today
spread out like a feast at a city that knows how to party,

at Fiesta Central at the corner of already and not yet, I want to say
*Look into the faces of those who love you*, those holy places
of *I'm so proud of you*, and take into your body memory,

your heart and belly, how this day feels.
Make the mornings count, today with its bright promise,
every day a slice of why not? I mean why can't you,

I know you can. It's the dress rehearsal for everything, and it's the show.
I want to send you safe and beaming into the next ten thousand mornings,
into the constant mountains and the meanings under the ravishing sky.

Into the arms of all who hold you and how you carry yourself.
Into the next and the best, not the last.  Into the endless nows
with their hard work and small pleasures, into the mystery

with its good news/bad news days. Into your one saved life,
your sacred breath and breathing. Into the Santa Fe you love
and the places that come after,

into the bring-it-on-I-can-take-it, I-can-make-it
city of no indifference, the intersection of all of us,
send you into the caring and daring new day.

## LOCKDOWN AT NAVA ELEMENTARY
## WHILE WE WERE LEARNING ALLITERATION

The school kids are used to the drama
drawn blinds, lights out,
while some crazed gun carrier cruises Siringo.

Nava being near
the high school is especially prone
to lockdown, lights out as the kids

were writing about traditions, the Quinceñera
with a last doll and Baille,
Family Night with Pizza.

The names of food shouted out
with sixth grade gusto, written on the board,
taco, posole, chimichanga, chicarrones, menudo.

meanwhile at the Round House, they repeal
driver's licenses for immigrants while people march
in protest outside .

Luckily my fever has gone,
but how the small terror alarms go off.
Last year a fire drill, these students so focused

and sweet, all writing poems as the dim day, for art,
that hidden door to the next room, the attic,
the basement, all of this before we are locked down.

The kids now under their desks,
now my fear rises for the bad hats out there.
For the pink clad, sneakered kids under their desks,

dark blinds drawn, locked down, my sweet old self.
Ms. Mayo shushing the kids,
poems in their blood streams, shush,

and the quiet in the room as soft as a quiet pet.
Shush, and the silence is cut darkly so sharply by
a sneeze, awesome alliteration in such sixth grade silence.

## Sixth Grade Continuation Ceremony at Nava Elementary

I will continue to be me, learning and yearning.
I will continue to live in this body my first home,
even as I grow older and bolder, taller and basketballer,
womanly and manly, even as I grow lumpy or grumpy,
I will still continue, changing shapes and landscapes,
to be me.

And I will learn. Every day I will continue to learn
new words for stars and movie stars, for green plants
and sidewalk ants. Maybe the names of trees
and the important honey bees, for French Poodles,
and snicker doodles. From hasta to pasta. Words
fly all around me and I will write them all, big
and small, chico y grande, words for
planets and hamsters and ham sandwiches,
chimichangas and empanadas and tamales
and through all the words I will continue to be me.

I will be the best me, more than all the rest.
I will continue to remember the good things
and forget all the pests. I will continue to run,
to jump rope, catch balls, hula hoop, and have fun.
I will fill water balloons and read under the good
and changing moon. I will continue to be fun.

And If I work hard doing what I love,
if every day I continue to read hard, to learn a little,

to kick a soccer ball until my muscles burn, if I continue
to study hard, nobody knows the rewards.
I will do art and be smart.  I will draw and paint
and nobody can say I can't. I will write another
poem, on any day good or sad.  I will be glad
to be continuously me.

So, I will be me and you will be you,
if you continue, if you really do,
remember  everything good you learned,
and follow, follow, follow through.
Continue, you and you and you,
the best you just might come true.

## North of Town

First day of snow
Read, then sew
Eat atolé
Talk on phone
No place to go

Late night in town
Stared my dreams down
Clouds implore, more
And more, then more
First draft, then encore

# DUE TO EXTREME PEACE THE MEMORY
# HAS BEEN CANCELLED

Today is a day I won't remember.
The guys at the rifle range practice
shooting. A plane doodles by leaving
contrails against the bluest sky.

The snow saying nothing
on the mountains.

I walk with my stick, and our white dog
who doesn't belong to us.  It's Christmas
and all day just the two of us.
Not sure if we are happy or lonely.

## KITCHEN SINK

Out my window I see sheep
growing their wool, their legs
more match stick every minute.  The view I can't see
of Truchas Peak because of the houses
and Russian Olive.  Birdfeeders three, thistle
and mixed seed, blue water bowl
hanging from the maple with no birds.
Garden where last summer K. and I met
the rattlesnake.  Now only kale
and carrots and arugula.  My car
because I am inside looking out
so always my silver Subaru
with its embedded story life.

Plenty O' Sky which would make
a nice name for a blue candy, similar
to Good 'N Plenty only blue mint
over a dark chocolate center.
The woodpile since it is now, but not if
it were last spring or next spring.

You might see K. in her pink fuzzy
jacket with hood because she is here.
There is a St. Francis statue with
the features wearing off, and a Jade
Buddha and the remains of all
the flowers that bloomed last summer.

Sparrows and house finches eating
the seeds that cause the Maximillian
sunflowers to list and sway. Piñon jay.
Compost pile. The dog, Cielo Acapella.
The moon at 2:00 PM.

What I don't see. Truchas Peak,
the town of Chimayo ten miles east
the holy dirt in the church, germs
which are invisible, lines of poetry.
Do you know that an apple to the earth
is the same as an atomic particle to something?
Musical notation, my back east family though I aim
for their hearts. No llamas, no alpacas, no cows
though there was a cow last year.
No clocks, no neighborhood. No library
among the *barrancas'* shelves.
No thunderheads or rain.
No cottonwood trees, though out back
there is a huge one, lightning struck,
*pobrecito,* and so we call it holy.
A man pulls up in a blue Chevrolet.
No more houseguests. Two men
smoking cigarettes from a blue pack,
American Spirits.

# GHAZAL

The bike tracks in the powdery dust, my boots, the various dogs.
Who is that black dog, another stray. I can't end this line with dogs.

On some level, I am a slave. On others ultimately free.
There is a strong connection between myself and our fine white dog.

We knocked back gratitude, got drunk on song, a loud cacophony.
Even our flawed notes are music, we howl like divine dogs.

Okay, he showed up, white and wild. All January, photos of wolves,
arctic scenes on calendars. I got the sense he was mine, dog.

I am a cat person, but the birds aren't. Neither are they against,
though our cat stalks them all the time, not our dog.

How did I get trapped in this endless ghazal. Blame the wind,
blame the music inside, or if there is a crime, blame the dog.

Okay, I have to admit I'm relieved the season has come but not yet
gone. Madame with five egos in Leo, you are going to shine like dogs.

Despite imminent war on Korean shores, why this joy?
Step back, step up, humans are a breed of march-in-line dogs.

Joni the pony has ridden off into sunset again and with rhyme.
Words like utterly and finale and sublime, we're God's dogs.

## Running Errands

The big snow
ruminating over the mountains
now descends

People walk with arms
open, make vertical snow
angels or maybe it's just us

Trying to outrun the snow's
huge flakes,  the city seen
through a veil

its natural glory in excelsius
all over me and you too, gifts
given in and out of offices

For lunch Bento boxes with
their compartments lose
to wood fired pizza

A thousand enchiladas sigh
a passel of chile rellenos
turn over on the stoves

You and I in this city
pretend we're on holiday
Twice you say, people

travel thousands of miles for this,
to sample saintly Santa Fe, simply
my decades of good luck

# Arrivistes

One hundred red winged blackbirds
heard the news, a panic of red flashes
emptying the feeders.  The snow.

I speak for the snow saying
*I am meant to be.  Stay home,*
*cancel your importance, trust*

*that the world will go on without*
*your expertise.*  The mountains
I live between, Sangres and Jemez,

these mountains speak to me
a stalwart and steady rim
to the west and to the east.

I am surrounded by bifurcated cold
and asked to find my ease. Finish
a book. Close its shiny covers.

Sleep under a sleeping bag
for extra warmth.  The blackbirds
promise me zero by New Year's Eve.

All the even numbers claim
zero as their own.  The odds
equally at home with nothing

and I tell you, zero will sting,
and our husky dog who sleeps
outside, will dream.  I'm seeing

the lengthening of days
past the eclipse I missed
due to clouds, lunar in shadow

solar, wind, snow, and me.
Today's note in the mail.
Thanking me for nothing.

There is nothing, nothing
that brings me happiness
like the red streaks in trees.

## LOS MATACHINES

He said, "Do you remember
that night in El  Rancho?"
insinuating there was something

to remember. He said, "Welcome
the newcomers. They are the heart also
of this valley."

The word Valley makes me
hollow so rivers can flow
in a time for rivers.

I have seen the snow
bless and bless the mountains
thirty seven times,

ten danzantes in ribbons,
and the Malinche all in white
the two abuelos, Montezuma.

We planted corn
when the thunderbird
disappeared from the mountain

I was here before the roads
were paved and yet
vague as a newcomer

this valley goes on before
goes on after, he points
to the sky just in case

someone, up there,
needs us.

## DRESSING DOWN FOR LOVE

Put on your love dress
take off your other garments
the ones that cost you most.
Wear your heart out.
Become a transvestite
for love. Cross dress as a heart.
Establish a municipality
with eyes you meet on the street.
Enter the election for darling.
Let kindness reign. Put
on no airs. Be plain as feet
which can also carry you away
along the Love Highway.
Hello. What is your name?
I have forgotten it. Remind me.

# WINTER POEM

His socks dry
hanging on a retablo
of Saint Michael.

When he leaves for town
and hardware, he says, See you
in the hereafter.

Every day I think
of death, of Eden,
of my three kids.

Yesterday I locked myself
in a courtyard of a pink church
with blue doors

and three feet of snow.
It was not a dream.

## President's Day

This weekend we spent together
forty one years ago, my hand
found its way into your back pocket,
blue jeans, Chicago rain, Zeller
Schwartz Katz. The lake raving
outside and down the block. It knew.
It certainly knew.

Tonight the driveway is awash
with flotillas of tumbleweeds
on the ocean of sandy soil.
Thirsty some years on the northern
Sonoran edge. The word edge
reasserts itself. Living here, hurricane force
with you, the hedges of tumbleweed
that throw themselves at our car, they throttle,
they menace, yet, barely and hardly.
They are as full of space as an atom.
They are scratchy as your beard,
as penetrable as thought, as hardly reliable
as a man with commitment issues.

I have been struggling with the giant tumbleweeds.
I am trying to say that they are as big, as what?
Smaller than a VW bug, larger than a dog.
Made mostly of space like matter, but stickery.
The Loch Ness Monster of desert.
But here we are on this lane.

All our days straddling me, all our nights
as slept off as anything. Pardon me,
I still have manners. But this morning
when the hurricane stilled and the sweat was over,

I thought of you working. The grace you have
on rooftops, at fence lines, with hands full
of wrenches and hammers and Leatherman,
that is your true elegance. I'm glad we had
this time together on the land. Don't think
of surprising me with ideas. You have
startled me with body, time and again.
The tumbleweeds today sit in scant calm,
they are just waiting for the next gust
to be on their way.

# STILL, LIFE WITH DATURA

She stepped out to pick the jonquils
a tame act along the edges of an illicit lawn,
a small patch of grass for the kids
and in those four strides out and four strides
back, managed to step on a seed pod
hiding in the grass, datura, at the corners
of their place to protect, fierce watch dogs
like gargoyles or the lions outside the NY public library,
or temple dogs. Inside her feet the seeds of datura lodged,
nothing unusual in this place of thorn and burr,
oh goat's head, red grass, stick⁄tight masquerading
in spring as beauty with tiny white flower, yucca sword,
pyracantha from the garden shop. Now this, grown from seeds
and into her foot they went and stayed.

Soon, as predicted from swallowed watermelon seed,
the warmth of her foot and moisture from her body
in this droughty spring, began to germinate the seeds
and a tiny pair of leaves emerged, one from each foot
not as in a painting of a woman with vines emerging
from her feet, but actual thick leaves, and she knew this
was a vision vine that could slay, stun, mock any
attempt at transcendence by undermining the day,
for she had heard. Yet she wore these feet aimed to flower,
Georgia O'Keeffe driving towards her in a car,
Tio Manzanares at the wheel, and paintbrush ready for white.
And that is how she finally landed, grounded in place

after transplanted three dozen years here, here, the woman
with datura in her blood, found in the tamest of setting.
She could not escape the wild.

## Camilla in the Afternoon

Just to meet at Black Mesa Golf course
with Sammy the Chihuahua, and your gift
of lineament for my bum ankle, the first time

since winter, just to meet. The acequia
brimming so full it's concave. Astonishing
mountain water. You say, "Thank you mama,"

blow kisses, and we take the acequia trail
and plan to come back in summer, ride
rafts down to the culvert.

Who cares if the golfers see us, we'll
cruise in style. I am already laughing
having a good time ahead of time

and you tell me the snakes swim upstream,
big ones with their heads above water,
but that doesn't scare me at all.

At the pond the koi have wintered over
they swim in the tumbleweed blown in,
a detail you point out and I have to steal,

lines so good, like your great aunt Mela
at one hundred, doing fine, and seeing
dead relatives in the garden in daylight.

Two little boys and her mother, who was
your great great-grandmother.
Aunt Mela. Any kin of yours is a force,

part of the land. Your book coming soon,
you worked so hard for it, putting Española
on the map. We talk about the old places

J.W. Owens and Emilio's, the restaurant
where the booths were shaped like a teepee,
a saloon, and church and a jail. Nobody

had those pictures and I didn't take them,
except in here, I point to my brain.
We get ice cream after. Only you

would like Butter Pecan, and I ask about gossip
forty years old. Dinah serves us, saving her tip
money for the trip to Spain. Elvis albums

on the wall, and a red and black tile soda
fountain, only she has no soda, no toppings
for sundaes, no cones, just Española

on Friday, two women who love the real.
I am ready to cruise the acequia, from
east to west, I am ready.

# DROUGHT

Fire season and we walk out of the Lensic
into haze, each street light ringed
like van Gogh or when I first wore
contact lenses. All the glare of air
kept me from vision.

Fire season waiting for monsoon
my husband drives into the mountains
with a friend and her daughter, daughter of
the woman I saw in the ground, can't talk about it
but after these weeks of smoke
rest in peace has a different ring to it.

My brother's heart in fire season,
a word I never spelled before, a stent,
like when we used to go camping in a tent,
you and I in the Maroon Bells
reading while it rained, an orange
plastic tube tent, and we had forty years

ahead, go figure, and how
would we know. Yesterday you asked
"How come you get to do that in poetry?"
It's the unconscious, I reply, a place
more worthy than I am myself. The underbrush,
the *coming in from under* said Kerouac,

the underworld. Can the unconscious
fall from above, like grace and angels,

or is it what Lorca meant? Duende, duende
duende in the afternoon.
How I feel about ash on the car
after it is washed, shiny, shiny

Fire season, this too shall, this too
shall, pass and ash have something in common.
How come you get to burn, fire?
No one can write a pre-
drought poem anymore.

## IMPERATIVE

I am having to write love poems
though the tree has been struck by lightning
the word "blighted" covers the landscape
and it hasn't rained in decades and yet
I am having to write love poems
as if words could save us

The rabbits have begun on the snapdragons
they already shredded the marigolds
and the Echinacea are only memories
and I am having to write love poems
Oh dearest one with your hem on fire
Oh darling let's order dessert
and have appetizers for the infinite

I am being called upon to write love poems
Sometimes an example of the beloved walks by
he is wearing a blue kimono
my friends have stopped speaking to me
because of all the publicity for the End Times
I have friended the Apocalypse on Facebook

The smoke is still over Raton Pass
and I am having to advance in this writing of love poems
Can you invent a new form? Can we resurrect
a morsel, a shred, a divot of vision?
The fault lines are groaning worldwide
the old poets gnashing their teeth

My dentist is reprimanding me for the like
and I say, give me new teeth
I have to write love poems
I can't be the poet laureate for springtime
I have to digest winter and chew on its ice
My dentist is aging but he is still filling

the rooms with laughter   He asked my daughter
when she was three, are you married? Now
this daughter is engaged and my dentist and I
know that the only way is to write love poems
Just imagine the gentle rain falling like heliotrope
Just imagine making love all night reciting

poems into the ear of the beloved  Just imagine anyone
could love that much and in what language  French?
Maybe if we spoke French we would have a love make-over
I have friended the Manhattan Project, brought it into
my own devices, the making of solar music
I have charmed the scientists, all of them

by reading love poems into their ears at night
as if the sleeping were more reasonable than the awake
and now we all have to recite love poems.

## SITTING STILL FOR BEAUTY

When I come into town, with my lists
and good outfits, with my parcels to mail
with my radio on KSFR. When I come into town
with its large art market, with its seven natural
food stores, with its plaza where they say
happiness hangs out, with its wide sidewalks
with its summer coming up bandstand, with
its built in fiestas and holidays, like a woman's
body. With its museums free on Fridays.

Coming into town with its spring wind
with its pollen counts piñon, mulberry, ash.
With its museums closed Monday
and in summer the Mountain Men come
and I always check on how Badger is doing
with his business card of leather. The Lensic
Theater reborn, that place I saw *Woodstock* in 1970.
Left the rainy screen for floods outside, waded,
made our way to camp at Hyde Park.

Here we are, part of the scenery, older
than we could have imagined. How place
agreed with us, wooed us, as we wooed
back. You worked for the state. I pollinated
the schools with poetry. We never know
the ripple effect of our efforts. And a woman
at an airport years ago said to somebody
with degrees of separation, "You have

Santa Fe hair." And I do, and inhabited
my sixth decade with a Santa Fe heart.

Drive, I say to my car. Holy city awaits you.
This week the 38th anniversary of arrival
once and for all, for better and for worse,
my other marriages to words and man.

# April in Santa

This is the city for poets. You'd think, Paris,
but I say here, just inside the library door
where magazines wait to be recycled into new
hands, where in the stacks the poets snuggle up

against one another, paperback by hard
cover, living by dead, they hum between
themselves, they speak in a frequency
heard only by readers.

And on the Plaza the poems wait
to be written down. They are suspended
in the air, a hacky sack flying from foot
to foot, a man looking down from a balcony,

a cash register tallying up the tax on a strand
of jewelry, liquid silver and jet. And the paintings
on the walls of the museums, or sculpture in gardens
just words away from saved and savored.

How this city is held afloat by art astounds
my lovely Wisconsin relatives held intact by
milk and road repair. They are driving off
with turquoise stud earrings for the granddaughters.

The birds bank and cycle above their rented car
and I am left here, my pen filled with ink
to immortalize, which means don't let this moment die.
City of poems, City of poets,

archiving the spring air, tracing the holy
pollen count which after all makes sacred seed of tree.
The birdsong of Thursday, the vibrations left in the
wake of artists who gather like iron filings

around this magnet of place. The ticket holders, the tourists,
the local girl who never went to a museum
before and now, skipping through bird and tulip,
it's her poem.

A little no capital letters e.e. cummings of a boy,
a large fat-lady-singing of a woman and this Opera is not over,
it keeps singing Spring, spring, spring and in Sena Plaza
the waiters can't help but burst Broadway

over the crowns of poppy waiting for their clock
of scarlet to tick open. On the Plaza my friend Sunny
selling glass earrings and barrettes. Have you noticed,
I mean how can you help but notice?

How many generations of souls from Santo Domingo
or Santa Clara sat under the portal through years and winters
for the arrival of April, in this holy city where April
is never cruel, though windy and more than deep.

Saint Francis making us all into instruments of His peace.
Poets accumulate to jot down the aha of place,
the jolt of jonquil, white bark of aspen, nuance
of sunset on the Cathedral.

Any place can be Paris, my old teacher said.
And in the library, I check out books, the delicate
arm of the librarian tattooed with apple blossoms.

## Poem Concerning Time

Written in conjunction with the Santa Fe Arts Commission
Community Gallery exhibit — *Mining the Unconscious*.
(After the monoprint "Tempest Fugit" by Sande Anderson.)


I see you, are like an eye
the numbers 22  23  24  25
like the tailor's tape measure
like a seamstress I never met

white shape cloud, cloth sky
I am a prayer for rain
I am only a prayer for rain
I am ageless as water before time

The background of my day
I am only a prayer for earth
I am wearing my father's skin
I am renting my mother's heart

if sheep could graze on me
if I held a flag
if the year 1982
meant my father was still alive

I am seeing you as you see me
we are only a waiting for water
we are silent until we run
we are empty and then we are emptier

I am pressed until the fiber
is woven into light
we are only a weave of air
we are only a prayer for rain

we are painted and then we dry
It could be 1982. It could be you.

# July 4

I am not patriotic
since I am a matriarch.
I can't help it, born female
in the old days, red white and blue
at birth and ever after.

I am saying gentle rain at the end
of every e-mail, every thought.
I am watching the clouds
wondering are you smoke
from the fires or moisture?

Red white and blue, I am
not patriotic, I love New Mexico
thirty eight years and my children
and my children's children born here.
I am praying for rain as I cook
as I try to grow anything.

The sky is filled with haze
there's a fire to the east and poems to the west.
There are fires to the south in small towns
I don't know. It's a new thought,
drought and ought.

# Free Friday Night in Santa Fe

"When I paint, I am trees."
*Georgia O'Keeffe*


In out of the trauma of the fires.
Two weeks, no, a month of smoke.
Three months of wind, inner space
invited me, isn't so bad.
There is a wind that blows
clear from Mexico and into Canada.
The birds know. Where do my hummingbirds
come from?

What woods burn while we watch
slides of trees? Saddest eyes
of this lung heart day.
There is sweetness in the air.
I was praying for gentle rain
and I got monsoon. I will settle
for flood, for roads impassible
and power outages. I will settle
for the army of ants who march
one by one as in a children's song
if tonight there is no fire creeping
down the canyon, the ridge, the ring
the steady march of flame, the scorch
of heat when I cannot write a thing.

Today I drew a tree for the ones lost
and I drew for the first time rain drops

those soggy cliché tears and between
prayer season and climactic change it worked
the rain rallied and fell, hail followed.
You were out in the wild lightning.

I was recalling when you walked
to the barn through blizzard. Here we are,
powerless as before but metaphors
grow literal on this land, this running
race with death, this dust garden, heat storm
night with nothing lit. No water in the sink
just run off and dark sky. But I'd trade it all
if little Santa Clara, holy place, now has
extinguished fire, if what is left is fine.

## FOURTH OF JULY

I managed to squeeze the day dry
love everywhere I looked on the Plaza
My two grandkids at pancake breakfast
and then home tonight
and the blaze is bright as before
squeezing its way down the canyon
in a flaming V. The girls and I walk
down to the arroyos mud, a small
stream of milky brown
and in the half life and half light
we soak our feet
the bright west eludes rain
the bright night in flame
so tears are clogged, so rain
must come. So anybody's game.

Today I scoured the news
16,000 acres in the Canyon.
If you've met the children of a place
you have seen its soul laughing.

Today we eat bread from the oven of friends.
I wrote poems with their daughter
a bright child who is now married,
shining, bride and bread.

I watched the moon turn off the light
I watched the sun go red. I saw a horse

watch the explosion over Jemez
just last Sunday.  He stared at the red-eyed sun.

We drive through blue smoke, under white
clouds and red flame. We stop at Camel Rock.
We stop at Nambé. The flags I fly are prayer flags.
How many tears will seed the clouds?
This is only a prayer for rain.

# Rain Business

The rain is not busy being rain
it is in business, raining, but not
busy. The rain falls on the cupola
I am sitting dry under rain.

Today I realized I am in dread
of weather. I drove the highway north
when fire exploded by Tesuque.
I drove south when the Jemez erupted.

Fire has a busy life, torching trees.
It is amoral. It is not altruistic.
It hates to be personified. *Yo Fire*
it never says to another flame.

I am busy worrying and obsessing.
Today's topics include arroyo flood
lightning when I drove to the pool
turned around and drove home unswum.

I am worrying about Republicans
and deficits. The Serenity Prayer is fine
but I am supporting the economy by worry.
I cannot do anything, but I can obsess

which is something. The rain doesn't default.
It stops. It just does its dew point, cloud
thing. I don't pay attention to history
but I obsess about weather. If rain were busier

the drought might end. It needs a day-planner,
it needs a wake-up call from the concierge of rain.
Wash your car, go to opera, hang out
lingerie hand washed.

Water the plants by hand, by dishwater.
Rain is not vain, but try placing mirrors
in the yard to reflect sky. If I could be tidy,
not slacker but efficient, if I could be rain.

I thought it would take all our tears.
I thought we would assemble teacups
in a row. I thought we would be leisurely,
weave hammocks of wind and light.

If all the sky looms in the west finally touched
the ground. Rain would fall. Sweet rain
with its gray leisure suit. Solid rain, clapping
for an encore. Dervish rain in white robes and turban,

and weather would not be the enemy.
Gratitude to the stunning relaxed rain.
trooping over the parched hills, good soldiers
of water, peace-making force against dusty armies.

## BESIDES FIRES

Besides fire, it's the season
of mothers' deaths and moving.
And in the moving and shifting,
monsoon bearing ash down
the Rio, our place is giving
the illusion of solid ground
so people store things,
for later or the Flea. Just wait
till you come back for your loom,
the hand woven shawl I resurrect
from solid dust, baptismal dresses
and wedding albums go, a Buddha
stays, a café table and chairs you
paint sea foam, books and white
plates so now I have twenty three.
And now the living creatures
that require care, a huge Norfolk
Island Pine, several jades and aloes,
wandering Jews, three peyote,
nobody is complaining, night blooming
cereus is a gift, those vines that like dark,
and one gorgeous bougainvillea
which already lost its flowers
in my care. My daughter's pit bull
is coming for a week, and two
miniature horses, not the stallion
who kicks and bites, but mares
falling in love with the neighboring

Mexican horses in the next stall.
All of this as we age and hope
to lighten up, imagine that.

# Visiting Placitas

when she dances you don't see
her widowhood, her Harvard
education

All evening
so stuffy we didn't see
the large fan

Already hot
for walking we didn't see
Larry Goodell's house

Passing the church
we could see roses lining
the walk, not prayers

Open every drawer
we could not see forks
for the life of us

Didn't see at first
the tiny book
I left last time

Lee Conner (the dancer) died
upstairs of AIDS
We didn't see it

When we were young
we couldn't see
this happiness now

# Waste

I told her, waste is part
of life.  The restaurant throws out
bags of rotten lettuce.
The ice box pays a toll, it tithes.
This I said in her car a year before her husband
died, grande mal of waste.

Today we saw a snake in the hencoop
wrap its mouth around a brown egg, too big
to fit, it unhinged its jaw

but still the good brown egg
stayed put.  Until, and we have photos
to prove it, it left the scene.
It was a coach whip I think.
You think, no, bull snake.  You and I
waste days after day in bickering.

The day before our 40th anniversary.
We never know if we'll make it one more.
Waste, and then you realize your drill

was stolen at the brick yard
on a job.  I got a parking ticket.
Now I can't find it and waste minutes
riffling though papers for a bright yellow
packet.  And how I've let my body
go and how you smoke at lunch.

Back to my own tenet.
We are alive and wasted.  Nothing.
Every morsel of zero or absence or

slacker or down time or wastrel, serves.
I weave the white of my hair
out of the clouds.  I drove an angel
down St. Francis Drive until my face
was white with winter.  I rode a pick-up
into the arroyo to gather white rocks.

I faced the algebra and geometry
of my family and washed all the numbers
and lines until my heart was white with love.

# THREE PARTS HARMONY

I.

Double rainbow off the back porch
dog wagging its ears on the front portal
10,000 hours is all it takes
to do the cha cha cha

Ten thousand hours on the phone
ten thousand at the store
meanwhile my words are taking time off
It's August in New York all across America

I used to be Chinese, I was Mongolian
like you. I used to be Persian
with a double rainbow to my right
and China if you dig deep. I used to be

awake, long before I fell asleep. Apart from that
it's chill. There ice making crystals in the frig.
There's that pesky rainbow scandalizing the sky.
There's gold buillon and the price keeps rising

and rising. The Indians are packing up from Market.
It's not called Native American Market or Indigenous.
It's Indian Market in Santa Fe and no one is wearing turquoise.
The tourists have forgotten how to dress, or maybe
it's the afternoon lot. Maybe the turquoise came and went.

My hummingbirds like the smell, the rainbow is off
the hook. I open up a chapter, my first sit down
all summer with your Neruda and Gerald Stern.
The men are all 83, every last beautiful one.
They are my dreamboats and my darlings.

Rain on the mental roof. Sun in the corner
of my eye, bullet proof  clouds and a paisley sky.
I never said that word. I never ever lied.
Sun on a cool tin roof. Rainbow on the sly.


2.


All summer I have been praying,
my biggest praying after the fires
burned and the smoke and ash,
after the one flood when the road ran
like Deer Creek. And now it is here
in my voice and on the roof, gentle gentle
rain. I forget what the prayer is for a prayer
answered. Is it thank you a thousand times
or some Hebrew words exact to the occasion
of rainbow, hummingbird madness, and rain?

3.

I think this is the most perfect day of my life.
Three days from my birthday, I drank sake
drove safely, now it is raining and I read.

I'm terrified to say that, raised on the *kineahora*
or evil eye, as I was.  Not my mother,
she was modern and an optimist, who then
gave me this dread of happiness?

This little wind⁄up anxiety when the toy factory
implodes and the joy runs down like a music box
with the pop⁄up ballerina.  There's a spider
ascending a strand of its own web. I wish

I could spin a little thread and navigate
vertically like my old teacher said.  Instead
I scan the horizon, I never send out for Chinese
food because nobody but the spider delivers

out here in La Puebla. I never send to the New
Yorker or even follow my prayers up.  Now
at last after months of saying it out loud, gentle
rains, antidote for drought, horizontal medicine.

I see a bird feed another large bird.  Is it courtship
or parenting? The slower the rain the deeper it falls
into this parch, three days before my birthday
perfect as it has been.

# GOODY TWO SHOES, A SONG LOOKING FOR A TUNE

Patti Smith cut the cuffs off her shirt
I would never do that, I would never do that
Our friend Webb went AWOL from Vietnam
we hid him out. Now, I would never do that.

Other people were dancing rock and roll
I was peeling the bark from a Ponderosa Pine
I was giving birth in a three-room house
with no running water and a full moon bass line.
Would you ever do that, would you ever?

The parrot ran off with the day
I would never do that, I would never do that
The magpies were making raucous hay
Their tuxedos and tails, their noisy ways

My mother was paying the bills, and soon
she'd be selling the shop.  The photos
of movies stars would fall. All would
vanish from the Carlton House Hotel.

Imploded by the imploding Italian brothers
we don't have it no more, it's gone.
I said, Hey Lovey Dovey,
yes I said, Hey, Lovey Dovey

We've been married these fast forty years
with our burgeoning  bourgeois frames
and our bank roll in your back pocket.
I'd never do that, you know I'd never.

Bob Dylan was passing through but I never got
his name. Janis Joplin would soon be through
and nobody called her tame. I put on my goody two shoes
and stared out the window in flame.

I gave birth to you and you and you
and nobody called out my name. I was Mama
I was Joanie I was Jane. I wore out
my Goody two shoes, I was wild and then I tamed.

You were tame and then you got wild.
Three times I handed you a child.
Just check it out, over here, all alone
It's Paradise without a throne.

Six acres and my last good nerve
Patti Smith came back in a huff
I rolled up my shirt cuffs. I deposited notes
in the bank, gave myself a third chance.

The small coyote danced, the computer
ran out of ink. The latest was just a child
with a heart as deep as the sink.
I can't stop finding the joy,

even when the meanings run out.
The evening was alive, it was evening's turn
to shout. I won't ever do this
I won't ever…I said Hey Lovely Dovey, said Hey…

# Unpunctuated Awe

*for WS Merwin*


So beautiful today
I don't know what to do with it
I can't be outside it's too perfect
the morning glories are too too without
even ingesting their known iota of trip
The Maximillian sunflowers are poised
to bloom and even that potential is wildly
enticing into too beautiful The dues we paid
After the fires after the wind and smoke the terrible
canyon fires of Santa Clara watershed tears shed
I could cry again today for the world we earned
paid its dues to too beautiful too beautiful
beautiful datura beautiful the Jewish New Year
I am already lamenting I stand naked for an hour
in my greenhouse watching the cereus flower
prepare for night blooming I stand naked before
my shower and after my shower  another phone call
from the too beautiful  I talk naked on the phone
because I don't know how to manage today
with how I love too beautiful the note in the mail
from you how I love poets and painters who make
the world shine me I never want to set foot
inside a classroom with no windows
I want to speak poetry to those finches
and to the kale I will tell the kale I forgive the aphids
you are so greenly beautiful I love my body today

because it is the vessel that carried too beautiful
soon departing for other beauty don't mention
it you say but in the too beautiful death
is already sharpening its scythe on too beautiful
its harvest of basil scent of mint too many
tomatoes and a glut of cucumbers and I forget
that I know how to preserve   I am doing it now

# AT GATHERING FOR MOTHER EARTH

*for Tewa Women United, written on site*

The corn is singing
all colors of corn are singing
and we are listening.

The sun is singing
the sky is blue singing
to all manner of listening.

The listening when
we don't even know
we are listening.

The distracted ear
The earth is listening
are we hearing?

The ground is the best
listener I ever knew
listening to fire and to rain.

My children teach me how to thank.
The jars of peaches, honey, jam
The elk in the freezer.

The three sisters, corn and beans
and squash are gossiping
about the weather.

The squash I didn't grow
my children grew,
planted ancient seed,

watered and now I carry
a large squash home. I guess
the children have been listening.

The grandkids have their fingers
on remote and I‑phone.
I am nearly giving up

but I have to believe
that they are listening.
The body listens

to the beautiful.  It feeds on
the horizon, a day like today,
a sun baked, heart based

day like today.

# THE SUBJECTIVITY OF IMPORTANCE

We make these lists and lose them
grout the tile, coffee, meeting in town.
Town is always Santa Fe, except
when it's Española except when
Monday rolls around and it's Halloween
Market. Last day of the season.
I mingle with farmers, some so old
that I look young. Today the four *viejos*
playing music the Smithsonian would love.
I sit inches from them, soaking music,
before I buy onions from Salvador and
Mr. Merhege who was principal
when I was substitute. Yellow apples.
This is the most important thing
I could be doing. The best place to spend.
Fix roof. Sort papers OJ yogurt bread
I have earned this ease, this sitting
among the elders, Esperanza, Sabra, Lucy
and Peter, peers, and Judy dresses as a witch,
Robin who drove me here from Chicago,
shows up in rubber mask and jelaba.
List: Thank you  You're welcome  Bring
in geraniums.  Parsley.   Dream.

# JACK GILBERT COMES TO THE LENSIC

In my dream, and I tell him how happy I am
to be the poet laureate, and he smiles with a sincerity
I doubt and claps my back, in hand a cigarette waiting
to be lit. But that is after I had forgotten
to publicize the reading of the two of us
and after I had forgotten to bring my poems
which mention Jack Gilbert and his old friend
and Pittsburgher Jerry Stern, I just didn't spend
a minute in preparation which is like me.
So I redeem myself, get the scraggly audience
to move forward in the ornate theater
tell people to Tweet their friends, it's not
too late. And I read with Jack Gilbert,
another Pittsburgher, after an odd day
of Pittsburgh connections, the old city
following me around like a pet owl.

# AFTER "THE MESA THE SHADOW BUILT"

Collage by Charles Greeley inspired by Judyth Hill's poem.


I wanted to sit by your feet, feed you
soup or that lamb and green chile,
mint jelly. Remember? The mesa is
dark and flowered, floral is another way
to say it, only mesas are dirt and tuff,
sandstone, not drilled by flowers.

Did the prayer work,
you and I concocting blessings? I am sitting
at the foot of your mountain and a river made
of origami paper and then a yellow bed of sand.
And love, how does love figure into it?
There are so many layers, some curved

some sharp, the insulation of beauty
against a fever of beauty. It is painful
yet the green layer struggles up,
there's still the green layer.
I sit at the foot. Remember the birth of Hope,
when you got in close with a camera?

I sent you to make grape juice. We had chocolate cake
and champagne though I asked for tequila.
That river between Pedernal and Mexico.
We sat at the foot of our old teacher. Nobody understood
him like we do. Nobody reads colors like you do.
You can see a metaphor just opening one eye.

I am cheating. We steal lines from one another.
There are doorways that say welcome in any language.
There are signs that say Do Not Enter.
Please enter again. I think you are able
to live in the haiku sky, the origami flowers
to gold language of Japan with its unaccented syllables.

# Occasional Poem

*From the stars in the heavens*
*I had to take two down*
*One to greet you*
*Another to bid farewell.*
*Four doves flew*
*Through all of the cities*
from LAS MAÑANITAS


Rodin sent Rilke out into Paris
to get out of his own head.
At the zoo he faced the panther,
its lope and grace confined.
At the foot of Archaic Apollo he knew
his life must change.

St. Francis sent me out into his city
to places and occasions I would ordinarily
miss. My hands writing everything down
in the noon glare. In Lensic dark
I took notes. You were there beside me
dear friend. We live as if our hearts
and art could change places.

This is the last occasion, Santa Fe.
*These are the dawns*
*that King David sang about.*
Back to the personal, back to the deep
waters of grief and family, wars unending

and evening news.  Back to the soles of
my feet on the dance hall floor, still
missing the beat, my voice that barely can sing,
"There's a hole in the bucket dear Henry"

and Las Mañanitas. *On the day that you were born
the flowers sang to you. On the day that you were born
the birds all sang to you.* I'll never look
at another city without a notebook and Rodin,
without Rilke, and all the poets here,
jotting noting writing brandishing a pen.
*All flowers were born on the day
that you were born*

This occasional life.

# ELECTION DAY AND VENUS TRANSITS THE SUN

Always vote for Venus,
This ain't our first rodeo.
Little boy at the Ranchitos pool
his mother calls, Romeo Romeo
Sponge Bob bathing suit
never has the blues looked so cute.
Tell him, Romeo and Venus
will grow up to elope.

Election day and this ain't
our first rodeo.  Our friend at the polls
had 48 weeks of chemo.
The other one lost his hair in a girlie show.
Always vote for Venus, you know
it ain't our first rodeo.

Everyone's dying, or else their wrinkles glow.
Living below this factory for Pluto
was just where my life lined flowed.
I'm a fool pessimist and an optimist
lying low.  And forget about context
this ain't our first rodeo.

My neighbor lingers in palliative care.
Three hippies at the ball game shared the one wheelchair.
 My friend in chemo still has all of his hair.
This may give him a third chance,
I'd follow him to any dance

You know the ballot's cast for Venus
and this ain't our last rodeo.

The harmonica and the Jemez are on fire.
The television shows are spitting out liars.
The radio has its program *Singing Wire*.
Fire in the Gila, tears can't put it out
cause this ain't our first Romeo.

Vote for Venus, cast your glance at fate.
The two of them out on an awkward first date.
Romeo and Venus dance on the blade of a knife.
You're in the ICU fighting for your life.
Walk on the wild side cause this ain't our first rodeo.


It's your movie so you get to dress for the role.
Handlebar mustache on every cowboy you know.
Living on Dead Thief Road, trespassers will implode,
cause we're living for Venus and this ain't our first rodeo.
Yes, we're voting for Venus and it ain't our last — Romeo.

# Blue Collar Holiday

At Capital Scrap Metal
you with three left gloves
in the Chevrolet truck. Me
missing my lipstick I left
in another pocket.
In the roaring clank of scrap
I am a devotee of recycle.
You with three right gloves missing.
Me with empty lips.

## INDIAN MARKET

Are you with me?
All the jewelry is taken out of the drawers
I have been commissioned by the city to fall in love,
and let me tell you it's not difficult.

I've seen a bunch of convertibles out on the highway
and the song "Indian Car" grabbed me from the radio
and forced me to cruise the Plaza for a parking space
which I found, can you dig it, and I can walk and write

and in a gallery my daughter pours bubbly water.
And on the plaza people dance the old hippie style,
loose and true in long skirts and native girls smile
that polite smile at an old white haired woman

writing standing up as the light from bright to mute moves
across the Cathedral.  Come winter, the shadow of a pine tree,
have you seen it, steals across St. Francis?

Got daffodils,
bought some pansies,
working on poems,
life is good and the turkeys are
singing a spring song.

# Gratitudes:

Thanks fly over our heads, especially where a series of places are listed. But I ask you to take these to heart:

The Santa Fe Arts Commission for the Poet Laureate Program, Sabrina Pratt, Debra Griego, and Julie Bystrom. Rod Lambert of the Community Gallery brings his amazing expertise to each gallery project. Thanks to Marilyn Batts who was an early PL mover and shaker as an arts commissioner. Thanks to others who have served on the Santa Fe Arts Commission.

To Arthur Sze and Valerie Martinez, the first two Santa Fe laureates, who paved the way and offered advice.

The Press at Palace of the Governors, Tom Leech and James Bourland, setting letters by hand for poet laureate books, posters, and my new chapbook, *April in Santa.*

Witter Bynner Foundation for Poetry and Steve Schwartz for the spiritual and financial support to Poet Laureate among other projects. I wouldn't have had the life in poetry I have had without their support.

Personally, during my poet laureate tenure, the LEF Foundation and the Vessel Foundation, made it possible to say more yes and less no. Endless gratitude.

Thanks to Miriam Sagan and Renée Gregorio, the dos chicas who made life and books more possible.

To Amanda Sutton, poetry publicist, who knew who to call.

To my husband, Michael Logghe, thanks pal, for putting up with me and being my consort. You were as helpful and understanding as could be. We had total fun.

My brother and sister-in-law, Carl and Carol Slesinger, who have relentlessly helped from the Back East.

Joan Logghe was Santa Fe's third Poet Laureate, serving from 2010–2012. She has taught extensively and to all ages, from UNM–Los Alamos to Zagreb, Croatia and Bratislava, Slovakia. She has been on the faculty of Ghost Ranch since 1990 and has been poet–in–residence at Santa Fe Girls' School since 1999. Her awards include a National Endowment for the Arts fellowship in poetry, a Mabel Dodge Luhan residency, and many grants from Witter Bynner Foundation for Poetry. Some of her many books are *The Singing Bowl*, (University of New Mexico Press), *Twenty Years in Bed with the Same Man* (La Alameda Press), editor *Odes & Offerings* (Sunstone), and *Love & Death: Greatest Hits* (Tres Chicas Books) with Miriam Sagan and Renée Gregorio, winner of a New Mexico Book Award. The three of them also founded Tres Chicas Books.

PHOTOGRAPH OF AUTHOR: Alex Traube

OTHER TITLES BY TRES CHICAS BOOKS

*Rice*  Joan Logghe, 2004

*Water Shed*  Renée Gregorio, 2004

*Just Outside the Frame:*
*Poets from the Santa Fe Poetry Broadside*
edited by Miriam Bobkoff and Miriam Sagan, 2005

*Big Thank You*  JB Bryan, 2006

*Water Shining Beyond the Fields*  John Brandi, 2006

*The Sound a Raven Makes*
Sawnie Morris   Michelle Holland   Catherine Ferguson, 2006
WINNER OF THE 2007 NEW MEXICO BOOK AWARD FOR POETRY

*Gossip*  Miriam Sagan, 2007

*Pinning the Bird to the Wall*  Devon Miller-Duggan, 2008

*The Man Who Gave His Wife Away*  Tom Ireland  2010

*Love & Death: Greatest Hits*
Renée Gregorio   Joan Logghe   Miriam Sagan  2011
WINNER OF THE 2011 NEW MEXICO BOOK AWARD FOR POETRY

*my thinned-skinned wandering*  Piper Leigh, 2011

*Her Knees Pulled In*  Elizabeth Jacobson, 2012

*Dizzy Sushi*  Melissa J White, 2013

*No Small Things*  Michael G. Smith, 2014


All Tres Chicas Book titles are available directly
from the publishers
or on the web at Amazon.com
& Small Press Distribution at spdbooks.org

*Kali is an aspect of the great goddess Devi, the most complex and powerful of the goddesses. Kali is one of the fiercer aspects of Devi, but nonetheless as Shiva's consort, she represents female energy. Kali's aspect is destructive and all-pervading, as she represents the power or energy of time. Her four arms represent the four directions of space identified with the complete cycle of time. Kali is beyond time, beyond fear . . . her giving hand shows she is the giver of bliss. Because she represents a stage beyond all attachment, she appears fearful to us. So, she has a dual aspect— both destroyer of all that exists and the giver of eternal peace.*

THIS IMAGE IS FROM DRAWINGS BY WOMEN OF MITHILA, INDIA.